Women Who Shaped History

Sojourner Truth
Early Abolitionist

Joanne Mattern

Rigby

Sojourner Truth: Early Abolitionist
Copyright © 2002 by Rosen Book Works, Inc.

On Deck™ Reading Libraries
Published by Rigby
a division of Reed Elsevier Inc.
1000 Hart Road
Barrington, IL 60010-2627
www.rigby.com

Book Design: Erica Clendening
Text: Joanne Mattern
Photo Credits: Cover, pp. 5, 6 (inset), 10, 11, 13, 15, 16, 17, 18, 19 courtesy of the archives of the Historical Society of Battle Creek; pp. 6–7 Cincinnati Art Museum, Subscription Fund Purchase, photo by Tony Walsh; p. 9 Cindy Reiman; p. 12 Erica Clendening; p. 20 courtesy of NASA/ JPL/Caltech; p. 21 courtesy of the Klyne Esopus Historical Society Museum

On Deck™ is a trademark of Reed Elsevier Inc.

07 06 05 04 03 02
10 9 8 7 6 5 4 3 2 1

Printed in the United States of America

ISBN 0-7578-2470-6

Contents

Isabella

Sojourner Truth was an abolitionist. She worked to end slavery. She wanted all people to be free and to be treated equally.

Sojourner Truth was born a slave around 1797 in New York State. Her name then was Isabella.

Now You Know

In 1806, Isabella was sold for $100.

When Isabella was 14, she married a man named Thomas. She and Thomas had five children.

In 1826, she ran away from her owners with her baby daughter, Sophia. She had to leave her other children behind.

Isabella's oldest child, Diana, was born in 1815.

A Quaker family took in Isabella and Sophia. Isabella took the family's last name, becoming Isabella Van Wagener.

Some people helped slaves become free.

Freedom!

In 1827, New York State freed the slaves living there. However, Isabella's six-year-old son, Peter, had been sold as a slave to a man in Alabama. It was against the law in New York to sell a slave to someone in another state.

Isabella and the Van Wageners went to court to get Peter back. They won! Isabella was one of the first African American women to ever win a court case.

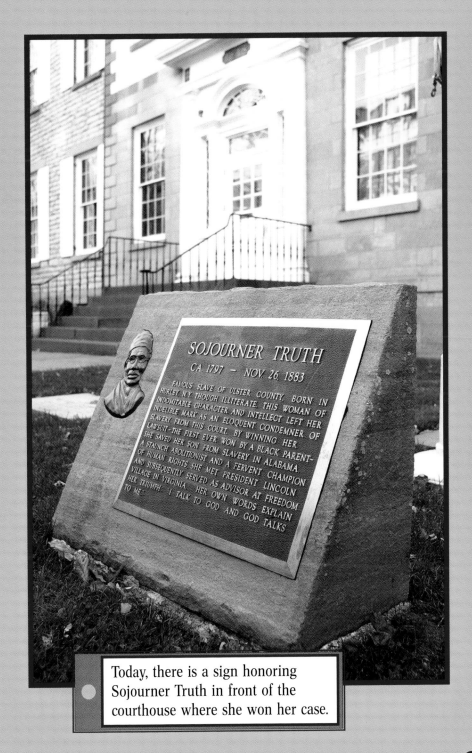

SOJOURNER TRUTH
CA. 1797 — NOV. 26, 1883

FAMOUS SLAVE OF ULSTER COUNTY, BORN IN HURLEY, N.Y. THOUGH ILLITERATE, THIS WOMAN OF INDOMITABLE CHARACTER AND INTELLECT LEFT HER INDELIBLE MARK AS AN ELOQUENT CONDEMNER OF SLAVERY FROM THIS COURT. BY WINNING HER LAWSUIT—THE FIRST EVER WON BY A BLACK PARENT—SHE SAVED HER SON FROM SLAVERY IN ALABAMA. A STAUNCH ABOLITIONIST AND A FERVENT CHAMPION OF HUMAN RIGHTS SHE MET PRESIDENT LINCOLN AND SUBSEQUENTLY SERVED AS ADVISOR AT FREEDOM VILLAGE IN VIRGINIA. HER OWN WORDS EXPLAIN HER TRIUMPH: "I TALK TO GOD AND GOD TALKS TO ME."

Today, there is a sign honoring Sojourner Truth in front of the courthouse where she won her case.

Sojourner Truth

In 1829, Isabella and Peter moved to New York City. Isabella was very active with her church.

In 1843, Isabella changed her name to Sojourner Truth. *Sojourner* means "traveler." Sojourner traveled around the country, telling people what she thought was the truth. She often spoke out against slavery.

Sojourner Truth often spoke from this stand in her church.

Many people came to see
Sojourner Truth give speeches.
She became very well-known.

11

In 1844, Sojourner moved to Northampton, Massachusetts. She joined a group called the Northampton Association. They were against slavery. There, she met a woman named Olive Gilbert. Sojourner told Olive her life story. Olive wrote down what Sojourner said and then printed a book called *Narrative of Sojourner Truth*. Sojourner sold the book and pictures of herself to make money.

Northampton, MA

New York City, NY

Atlantic Ocean

Sojourner Truth lived in Northampton, Massachusetts until 1857.

NARRATIVE

OF

SOJOURNER TRUTH;

A Bondswoman of Olden Time,

EMANCIPATED BY THE NEW YORK LEGISLATURE IN THE EARLY
PART OF THE PRESENT CENTURY;

WITH A HISTORY OF HER

Labors and Correspondence,

DRAWN FROM HER

"BOOK OF LIFE."

BOSTON:
PUBLISHED FOR THE AUTHOR.

SOJOURNER TRUTH,
"THE LIBYAN SIBYL."

The story of Sojourner Truth's life was printed in 1853. Sojourner was about fifty-six years old.

Sojourner's Work

During this time in America, women did not have the same rights as men. For example, women were not allowed to vote. Sojourner gave many speeches to get women the same rights as men. At almost six feet tall, Sojourner used a strong voice and a sense of humor to get angry crowds to listen to her.

"Look at me! Look at my arm! I have plowed, and planted, and gathered [crops] into barns, and no man could [do better than] me. And ain't I a woman?"

—Sojourner Truth

FREE LECTURE!

SOJOURNER TRUTH,

Who has been a slave in the State of New York

Even though Sojourner Truth gave many speeches,
she never learned how to read or write.

During the time the Civil War was fought in America, Sojourner helped African American soldiers. She also went to the White House and met President Abraham Lincoln.

In 1865, the Civil War ended. Slavery ended, too. Sojourner helped slaves who were freed. She helped them find jobs and places to live.

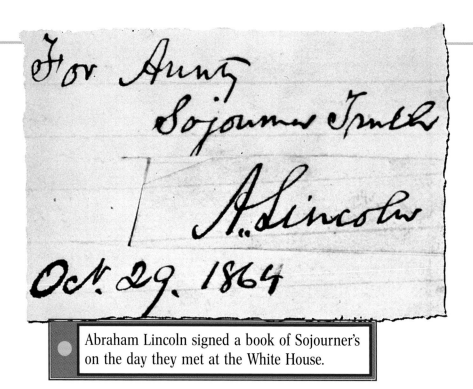

Abraham Lincoln signed a book of Sojourner's on the day they met at the White House.

This painting shows Sojourner meeting with President Lincoln.

17

The Final Years

Sojourner traveled and made speeches until she was about eighty-five years old. On November 26, 1883, Sojourner died at home in Battle Creek, Michigan. More than 1,000 people came to her funeral.

Time Line

1797 *Isabella is born*

1827 *Slaves are freed in New York State*

1826 *Runs away to live with the Van Wageners*

1828 *Wins a court case to get her son, Peter, back*

Sojourner Truth's home in Battle Creek, Michigan

Sojourner may be the most famous person to have ever lived in Battle Creek, Michigan. She is buried there, too.

1843 *Isabella changes her name to Sojourner Truth*

1864 *Visits President Lincoln in the White House*

1851 *Makes important speech about women's rights*

November 26, 1883 *Sojourner Truth dies*

Sojourner Truth fought for freedom for all people at a time when slavery was common. She also worked to get more rights for women and African Americans. Sojourner Truth will never be forgotten.

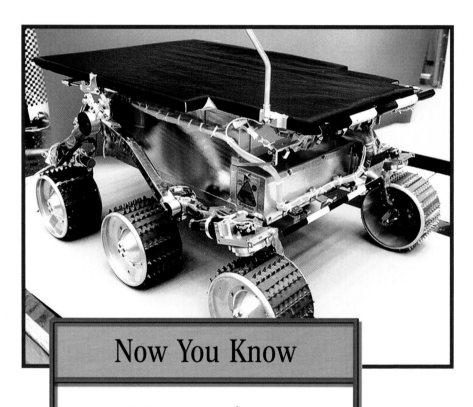

Now You Know

In 1997, a machine was sent to study the planet Mars. It was named *Sojourner* in honor of Sojourner Truth.

Sojourner Truth
22

Black Heritage USA

In 1986, a postage stamp was made to honor Sojourner Truth.

"It is hard for the old slave-holding spirit to die, but die it must."

—Sojourner Truth

Glossary

abolitionist (ab-uh-**lihsh**-uh-nihst) someone who works to end slavery

Civil War (**sihv**-uhl **wor**) the war fought from 1861 to 1865 between the northern and southern states of the United States

court (**kort**) a place where a judge decides questions of law

funeral (**fyoo**-nuhr-uhl) a service held in honor of someone who has died

Quaker (**kway**-kuhr) a Christian group

rights (**ryts**) things the law says that a person is allowed to do

slave (**slayv**) a person who is owned by another person and forced to do work

slavery (**slay**-vuhr-ee) the practice of owning people and forcing them to do work

soldiers (**sohl**-juhrz) people who serve in an army to protect a country and its belongings

Resources

Books

Only Passing Through:
The Story of Sojourner Truth
by Anne F. Rockwell
Alfred A. Knopf (2000)

Walking the Road to Freedom:
A Story about Sojourner Truth
by Jeri Ferris
The Lerner Publishing Group (1991)

Web Site

Sojourner Truth Institute
http://www.sojournertruth.org

Care was taken in selecting Internet sites. However, Internet addresses can change, or sites can be under construction or no longer exist.

Rigby is not responsible for the content of any Web site listed in this book except its own. All material contained on these sites is the responsibility of its hosts and creators.

Index